CW01086645

"漫画汉语101句"
系列丛书策划

周明伟　黄友义　徐明强
王君校　韩　晖

Chinese 101 in Cartoons

(For Students)

漫画汉语101句
（学生篇）

张 婧 陈晓宁 编著
J.Y. Standaert 译
黄钧升 插图

华语教学出版社
SINOLINGUA

First Edition   2009

ISBN 978-7-80200-628-7

Copyright 2009 by Sinolingua

Published by Sinolingua

24 Baiwanzhuang Road, Beijing 100037, China

Tel: (86) 10-68320585

Fax: (86) 10-68326333

http://www.sinolingua.com.cn

E-mail: hyjx@sinolingua.com.cn

Printed by Beijing Foreign Languages Printing House

Printed in the People's Republic of China

Preface

Due to the 2008 Beijing Olympic Games, China has become the focus of world attention. An increasing number of foreign friends are eager to know more about the country and communicate further with the Chinese people. The number of foreigners learning Chinese throughout the world is increasing on a yearly basis and "Chinese fever" is gaining momentum. Yet due to limitations of time and learning conditions, a large number of foreigners who want to learn Chinese still have no access to regular and professional training. There are also many people who simply give up because of the degree of difficulty involved. To resolve these problems and help assist those who basically have no knowledge of Chinese to master some words and expressions for everyday use, we have carefully designed this series, titled *Chinese 101 in Cartoons.*

Each book in this series is designed to cater to the various needs of different people. The 101 expressions selected are all used frequently in daily conversation. The series mainly has two features: the lively and colorful cartoons which help readers better understand the conversational scenes; the recording of standardized Mandarin Chinese, which is necessary to help develop the correct pronunciation. There is no obscure grammar here, and readers need not memorize the strokes of the Chinese characters. All they need to do is to imagine the scene with the aid of the cartoon, try to memorize the Chinese sentence with the help of the English translation, and pronounce it with the help of the pinyin and the recording.

In addition, there are many word options that can serve as substitutes for those in the 101 commonly used sentence patterns presented in each book. The learners thus can draw inferences about other sentences from any given example. There are lively and humorous tips with cartoons that introduce Chinese customs and culture, and also explain differences between the East and the West.

Catchy and lively Chinese conversation starts from *Chinese 101 in Cartoons.* With one book on hand, you can proudly say: "I can speak Chinese!"

前言

随着 2008 年北京奥运会的举办，中国已成为世界瞩目的焦点。越来越多的外国友人希望了解中国，渴望与中国人交流。在世界各地，学习汉语的外国人正逐年增加，"汉语热"持续升温。由于时间、条件等的限制，许多有学习汉语愿望的外国人目前无法在学校接受正规、系统的课堂教学；也有一些外国人认为汉语这门古老的语言难学、难记，难以掌握，对此望而却步。为了解决这些问题，帮助更多汉语为零起点的外国人学习一些简单的日常用语，我们精心策划了这套"漫画汉语 101 句"系列丛书。

丛书每册根据不同人群的不同需求分别编写，均选取日常会话中使用频率较高的 101 句话教给读者。以轻松活泼的彩色漫画形式帮助读者理解会话场景、以标准的普通话录音帮助读者模仿发音是本书最大的特色。在这里，没有生涩难懂的语法，不需要熟记汉字笔画，只需借助画面进入情境、根据与中文句子对应的英文理解意思、对照汉语拼音读出发音就可以了。

另外，每册书提供的 101 句常用句式同时给出了多种可替换词语，学习者可以举一反三，一句衍生多句。书中更有生动幽默、配漫画的小贴士介绍中国的风俗习惯、文化常识，以及中外差异趣闻等，帮助读者了解中国。

简单易学、生动有趣的汉语，从"漫画汉语 101 句"开始。一书在手，你就可以骄傲地说：我会说汉语了！

Key to Pronunciation

Beginning Consonants

b	*b* as in *be*
c	*ts* as in *tsar*, strongly aspirated
d	*d* as in *do*
f	*f* as in *food*
g	*g* as in *go*
h	*h* as in *her*
j	*j* as in *jeep*
k	*k* as in *kind*
l	*l* as in *land*
m	*m* as in *man*
n	*n* as in *nine*
p	*p* as in *par*
q	*ch* as in *cheek*
r	like *z* in *azure*
s	*s* as in *sister*
t	*t* as in *ten*
w	*w* as in *way*
x	*sh* as in *she*

y	*y* as in *yet*
z	*ds* as in *needs*
zh	*j* as in *jump*
ch	*ch* as in *church*
sh	*sh* as in *shore*

Vowels and Diphthongs

a	*a* as in *father*
ai	*i* as in *kite*
ao	*ow* as in *now*
an	*ahn*
ang	like *ong* in *song*
e	*er* as in *her* (Brit.)
ei	*ay* as in *way*
en	weak form of *an* as in *and*
eng	no English equivalent but nearly as *ung* in *lung*
i	*ea* as in *eat*
ia	*yah*
ie	*ye* as in *yes*
iao	*yow* as in *yowl*
iou	*yee-oh*

ian	*ien* as in *lenient*
in	*een* as in *keen*
iang	*i-ahng*
ing	*ing* as in *sing*
iong	*y-oong*
o	*aw* as in *law*
ou	*ow* as in *low*
ong	*oo-ng*
u	*oo* as in *too*
ua	*wah*
uo	*wa* as in *water*
uai	*wi* as in *wife*
uei	as *way*
uan	*oo-ahn*
uen	*won* as in *wonder*
uang	*oo-ahng*
ueng	*won* as in *wont*
ü*	as "*yü*" in German
üe	no English equivalent
üan	no English equivalent
ün	no English equivalent

---

* "ü" is spelt so only when it follows "l" and "n", while it is spelt as "u" in all other places.

目 录

第一部分　准备篇
Part 1　Preparing for School

Bǎoluó: Qǐngwèn nín shì x x Dàxué de lǎoshī ma?
① 保罗: 请问 您是 ×× 大学 的 老师 吗?

Paul: Excuse me, are you from XX University?

Jiē jī lǎoshī: Wǒ shì. Nǐ shì——
接机老师: 我 是。你 是——

Teacher at the airport: Yes, I am. And you are?

Bǎoluó: Wǒ shì Bǎoluó, cóng Měiguó lái.
② 保罗: 我 是 保罗, 从 美国来。

Paul: I'm Paul. I'm from the United States.

Jiē jī lǎoshī: Huānyíng nǐ, Bǎoluó!
接机老师: 欢迎 你, 保罗!

Teacher at the airport: Welcome to China, Paul!

Hánguó
韩国 Korea
Rìběn
日本 Japan
Yìndùníxīyà
印度尼西亚 Indonesia
Éluósī
俄罗斯 Russia
Jiānádà
加拿大 Canada
Àodàlìyà
澳大利亚 Australia
Bāxī
巴西 Brazil
Yīngguó
英国 United Kingdom
Fǎguó
法国 France
Déguó
德国 Germany
Hélán
荷兰 the Netherlands
Ruìdiǎn
瑞典 Sweden

bàomíng
报名 sign up
bàn shǒuxù
办手续 fill out the forms
dēngjì
登记 register
jiǎofèi
缴费 pay

Bǎoluó: Qǐngwèn zài nǎr zhùcè?
③ 保罗: 请问 在哪儿 注册?

Paul: Excuse me, where do I register?

Gōngzuò rényuán: Sān lóu C sān líng yī bàngōngshì.
工作 人员: 三楼C 301 办公室。

Staff: Go to office C301 on the third floor.

④
Bǎoluó: Xièxie!
保罗: 谢谢!

Paul: Thank you.

Gōngzuò rényuán: Diàntī zài zhè bianr.
工作 人员: 电梯在这边儿。

Staff: The elevator is over here.

> Lóutī
> 楼梯 stair
> Fútī
> 扶梯 escalator

⑤ Bǎoluó： Wǒ jiào Bǎoluó， wǒ lái zhùcè．
保罗： 我 叫 保罗， 我 来 注册。

Paul: Hello, my name is Paul, and I'm here to register.

Gōngzuò rényuán： Qǐng xiān tiánxiě zhèxiē biǎogé， ránhòu qù
工作 人员： 请 先 填写 这些 表格， 然后 去
xuéxiàocáiwù-chù jiǎo fèi．
学校财务处 缴费。

Staff: Please fill out these forms first, then you can go to the cashier's office to pay.

Bǎoluó:　Hǎo.　Kěyǐ yòng Yīngyǔ tián ma?

⑥ 保罗：好。可以用 英语 填吗?

Paul: Okay. Can I fill out the forms in English?

Gōngzuò rényuán:　Hànyǔ,　Yīngyǔ dōu kěyǐ.

工作 人员：汉语、英语 都可以。

Staff: You can fill them out in either Chinese or English.

Fǎyǔ 法语 French
Déyǔ 德语 German
Rìyǔ 日语 Japanese
Xībānyáyǔ 西班牙语 Spanish
Hányǔ 韩语 Korean
Ālābóyǔ 阿拉伯语 Arabic

Bǎoluó: Zhè shì shénme?
⑦ 保罗：这 是 什么？

Paul: What's this?

Gōngzuò rényuán: *Rùxué Shǒucè* hé zhè jǐ tiān de shíjiānbiǎo.
工作 人员：《入学手册》和这几天的时间表。

Staff: It's the *Student's Guide* and the schedule for the next couple of days.

⑧ Bǎoluó: Shénme shíhou kāixué?
保罗: 什么 时候 开学?

Paul: When does school start?

Gōngzuò rényuán: Jiǔyuè yī hào, xià
工作 人员: 九月一号，下
xīngqīyī.
星期一。

Staff: Next Monday, on
September 1st.

kāishǐ shàngkè do classes start
开始上课
kǎoshì do exams start
考试
hé Zhōngguó tóngxué liánhuān
和 中国 同学 联欢
do we get together with
the Chinese students

xīngqī'èr		xīngqīsān	
星期二 Tuesday		星期三 Wednesday	
xīngqīsì		xīngqīwǔ	
星期四 Thursday		星期五 Friday	
xīngqīliù		xīngqīrì	
星期六 Saturday		星期日 Sunday	

Bǎoluó： Nǎ tiān jǔxíng kāixué diǎnlǐ ne ?

⑨ 保罗： 哪 天 举行 开学 典礼 呢?

Paul: When is the opening ceremony?

Gōngzuò rényuán： Hòutiān .

工作 人员： 后天。

Staff: The day after tomorrow.

Jīntiān
今天 Today
Míngtiān
明天 Tomorrow
Dà hòutiān
大后天 Two days
after tomorrow

Student Years

Chinese children usually start school at the age of six or seven. Elementary education is usually six years. Middle school refers to junior high school and senior high school. It lasts a total of six years. After senior high school, most students go to university. Other students start work or go to vocational school. University is usually four years. Some particular majors, like medicine, can take up to five or six years. After graduating from university, some students continue on to graduate school for a Master's or PhD. Master's usually take three years and PhDs usually take three to six years. If you count the years of school beginning from the first grade, students can be close to thirty years old when they finally get their PhDs.

大学毕业纪念（22岁）

小学一年级纪念（6岁）

Fúwù rényuán : Qǐng chūshì nǐ de hùzhào

服务人员 : 请 出示 你的 护照。

zhèngjiàn
证件 ID
xuéshēngzhèng
学生证 Student ID

School personnel: Please show your passport.

Bǎoluó : Gěi nín.

⑩ 保罗 : 给您。

Paul: Here you go.

Fúwù rényuán : Zhè shì nín de fángkǎ .
服务人员 : 这是您的房卡。
School personnel: Here is your room card.

yào shi
钥匙 key

Bǎoluó : Fángjiān li kěyǐ shàngwǎng ma?
⑪ 保罗 : 房间里可以 上网 吗?
Paul: Can I get online in the room?

xǐzǎo
洗澡 take a bath
zuòfàn
做饭 cook
dǎ guójì chángtú
打国际长途
make international phone calls

Fúwù rényuán : Kěyǐ .
服务人员 : 可以。
School personnel: Yes, you can.

⑫ Bǎoluó： Shítáng zài nǎr ?
　　保罗： 食堂 在哪儿?

Paul: Where's the cafeteria?

Fúwù rényuán ： Gōngyù yī lóu jiù yǒu .
服务人员 ： 公寓 一楼 就 有。

School personnel: There's one on the first floor of the apartment.

Cānting
餐厅 restaurant
Zhōngcānting
中餐厅　Chinese restaurant
Kuàicānting
快餐厅 fast-food restaurant
Kuàicāndiàn
快餐店 fast-food store

食堂在哪儿?

公寓一楼就有。

⑬ Bǎoluó: Yǒu xīcāntīng ma?
保罗: 有西餐厅吗?

Paul: Is there a restaurant that serves western food?

Fúwù rényuán: Xuéxiào běi mén pángbiān yǒu yì jiā búcuò
服务人员: 学校 北 门 旁边 有一家不错
de xīcāntīng, duìmiàn háiyǒu Màidāngláo.
的西餐厅, 对面 还有 麦当劳。

School personnel: There's a good one next to
the north gate of the school.
And a McDonald's is right
across the street from it, too.

Kěndéjī
肯德基 KFC
Bìshèngkè
必胜客 Pizza Hut
Xīngbākè
星巴克 Starbucks
Sàibǎiwèi
赛百味 Subway
Jíyě-jiā
吉野家 Yoshinoya

有西餐厅吗?

学校北门
旁边有一家
不错的西餐
厅，对面还
有麦当劳。

⑭ Bǎoluó : Lǎoshī wǒ de chéngjì zěnmeyàng?
保罗：老师，我的 成绩 怎么样？

Paul: How is my score?

Lǎoshī : Hái búcuò .
老师：还 不错。

Teacher: Not bad.

kǎoshì
考试 test
shuǐpíng
水平 level
chéngdù
程度 level
fāyīn
发音 pronunciation
yǔfǎ
语法 grammar
zuòwén
作文 writing

Bǎoluó: Wǒ zài jǐ bān?
⑮ 保罗： 我 在 <u>几班</u>？

> nǎge
> 哪个 Which

Paul: <u>Which</u> class am I in?

Lǎoshī: Nǐ zài 4 A bān.
老师： 你 在 <u>4A 班</u>。

Teacher: You're in <u>Class 4A.</u>

> chūjíbān
> 初级班 the beginner's class
> chūjí xiàng zhōngjí guòdùbān
> 初级 向 中级过渡班
> the beginner's to intermediate class
> zhōngjíbān
> 中级班 the intermediate class
> zhōngjí xiàng gāojí guòdùbān
> 中级 向高级过渡班
> the intermediate to advanced class
> gāojíbān
> 高级班 the advanced class
> yùkēbān
> 预科班 the preparatory class
> yánxiūbān
> 研修班 the further education class
> yánjiūshēng1 bān
> 研究生 1 班 graduate Class 1

你在 4A 班。

我在几班？

Bǎoluó： Wǒmen yǒu shénme kè ?
⑯ 保罗： 我们 有 什么 课?

Paul: What classes do we have?

Lǎoshī： Zhè shì nǐ de kèchéngbiǎo .
老师： 这 是你的 课程表 。

Teacher: This is your schedule.

Bǎoluó: Jiàoshì zài nǎr a?
⑰ 保罗: 教室 在哪儿啊?

Paul: Where's the classroom?

Lǎoshī: 45 hào lóu 4 céng.
老师: 45 号楼 4 层。

Teacher: It's on the 4th floor of Building
No. 45.

Jiàoshī bàngōngshì
教师 办公室
teachers' office
Liúxuéshēng bàngōngshi
留学生 办公室
foreign students
office
Xuéshēng gōngyù
学生 公寓
student apartment

School Semesters and Holidays

In China, school semesters and holidays for elementary schools, middle schools, and universities are basically the same. A full academic year consists of two semesters. The first semester starts in September and ends in January of the following year. The second semester starts in March and ends in July. Between the two semesters is the winter and summer vacations. Students usually have many plans during the two holidays. Some go vacationing, some take part in community work, and some enroll in additional courses or programs.

Bǎoluó: Shì zài zhèr mǎi kèběn ma?
⑱ 保罗：是 在 这儿 买 课本 吗？

Paul: Do we buy our textbooks here?

Lǎoshī: Shì de. Nǐ shì nǎge bān de?
老师：是的。你 是 哪个 班 的？

Teacher: Yes. Which class are you in?

jiàocái
教材 teaching material
xuéxí cáiliào
学习材料 studying material
cídiǎn
词典 dictionaries
zìdiǎn
字典 dictionaries
cídài
磁带 cassette tapes
CD/DVD

⑲ Bǎoluó：　4A bān．Yígòng duōshao qián？
保罗：　4A 班。一共 多少 钱？

Paul: 4A. How much is the total?

Lǎoshī：　Èrbǎi líng èr kuài．Zhè shì fāpiào．
老师：　202　块。这是发票。

Teacher: 202 yuan. Here's your invoice.

shōujù
收据 receipt

Lǎoshī : Bǎoluó， zěnme le ?
老师： 保罗， 怎么了?

Teacher: What's the matter, Paul?

tīng bu qīng	
听不清	I can hear clearly
kàn bu dǒng	
看不懂	I can read properly
bù míngbai	
不明白	I understand
bù qīngchu	
不清楚	it's clear to me

Bǎoluó : Lǎoshī， wǒ yǒudiǎnr tīng bu dǒng。
⑳ 保罗： 老师， 我有点儿 听不懂 。

Paul: I don't think I understand everything.

Lǎoshī： Bié zháojí ． Nǐ yǒu shénme xiǎngfǎ？
老师：别着急。你有 什么 想法？

Teacher: Don't worry. What would you like to do?

Bǎoluó： Wǒ xiǎng huàn ge bān．
㉑ 保罗：我 想 换 个 班。

Paul: I'd like to change classes.

Lǎoshī : Nà jiù qù 3 B bān ba .
老师： 那就去 3B 班吧。

Teacher: You can go to 3B then.

Bǎoluó : Hǎo de， wǒ qù shìshi .
㉒ 保罗： 好的，我去试试。

Paul. Okay. I'll give it a try.

那就去 3B
班吧。

好的，
我去
试试。

The Longest and Shortest

A teacher asks his students, "What is the longest thing in the world and what is the shortest thing in the world?"

A student answers, "The last minutes of a class are the longest, and the last minutes of an exam are the shortest."

第二部分 学业篇
Part 2 Studies

Bǎoluó : 3 B bān dōu yǒu shénme kè ?
㉓ 保罗: 3B班 都 有 什么课?

Paul: What courses do you have in 3B?

Lǎoshī : Bìxiūkè yǒu zhōngjí Hànyǔ, kǒuyǔ hé zhèngyīn, yuèdú
老师: 必修课有 中级 汉语、口语和 正音 、阅读
hé xiězuò, zhōngjí tīnglì. Zhè shì kèchéngbiǎo.
和写作、中级听力。这是 课程表 。

Teacher: Required courses include Intermediate Chinese,
Conversation and Pronunciation, Reading and Writing,
and Intermediate Listening. This is the schedule.

Bǎoluó: Wǒmen yǒu xuǎnxiūkè ma?
㉔ 保罗： 我们 有 选修课 吗?

Paul: Do we have electives?

Lǎoshī: Yǒu hěn duō xuǎnxiūkè, bǐrú Zhōngguó wénhuà, tàijíquán,
老师： 有 很 多 选修课, 比如 中国 文化、太极拳、

shūfǎ. Hái yǒu jiǎngzuò, fǔdǎo hé yǔyán shíjiàn huódòng.
书法。还 有 讲座、辅导和语言实践 活动 。

Teacher: There are many electives, such as Chinese Culture,
Tai Chi, and Calligraphy. There are also lectures,
guided courses, and language-in-action activities.

Bǎoluó： Tài hǎo le !
㉕ 保罗： 太 好 了！

Paul: Sounds great!

Lǎoshī :　Bǎoluó，qǐng xiàng dàjiā jièshào yíxià　zìjǐ .
老师：保罗，请 向 大家介绍一下自己。

Teacher: Would you please introduce yourself to everyone, Paul?

Bǎoluó :　Dàjiā hǎo !　Wǒ shì Bǎoluó，láizì Měiguó，hěngāoxìng
㉖ 保罗：大家好！我 是 保罗，来自美国，很 高兴
rènshi dàjiā . Wǒ hěn xǐhuan Hànyǔ hé Zhōngguó wénhuà .
认识大家。我 很 喜欢 汉语和 中国 文化。

Paul: Hello everyone! I'm Paul and I'm from the United States. It's a pleasure to meet you. I like Chinese and Chinese culture very much.

Zhōngguó wénxué
中国 文学 Chinese literature
Zhōngguó shūfǎ
中国 书法 Chinese calligraphy
Zhōngguóhuà
中国画 Chinese painting
Zhōngguó xìqǔ
中国 戏曲 Chinese opera
Zhōngguó gōngfu
中国 功夫 Chinese martial arts
Zhōngguó měishí
中国 美食 Chinese food

保罗，请向大家介绍一下自己。

大家好！我是保罗，来自美国，很高兴认识大家。我很喜欢汉语和中国文化。

The Curriculum

The university curriculum in China consists of required courses, elective courses, and practicum courses. Students must fulfill all the course requirements in order to graduate. They must present a graduate paper or project upon graduation and defend it in front of a school committee.

Lǎoshī : Qǐng jìn !

老师： 请 进！

Teacher: Please come in.

Bǎoluó : Duìbuqǐ , wǒ lái wǎn le .

㉗ 保罗： 对不起，我来晚了。

Paul: I'm sorry I'm late.

Zhēn bàoqiàn
真 抱歉 I'm really sorry
Shízài bàoqiàn
实在 抱歉 I'm really sorry
Zhēn bù hǎo yìsi
真 不好意思 I'm really sorry

Bǎoluó： Lǎoshī， nín néng zài shuō yí biàn ma?
㉘ 保罗：老师，您 能 再 说 一 遍 吗?

Paul: Excuse me, Mr. X, can you

say it again?

chóngfù
重复 repeat

Lǎoshī： Qǐng tīnghǎo ...
老师： 请 听好……
Teacher: Listen carefully.

Bǎoluó： Lǎoshī， nín néng shuō màn yìdiǎnr ma?
㉙ 保罗： 老师， 您 能 说 慢一点儿吗?

Paul: Mr. X, can you say it a little
bit slower?

kuài yìdiǎnr
快一点儿 faster

Lǎoshī： Hǎo de .
老师： 好 的。
Teacher: Sure.

Bǎoluó： Lǎoshī， nín gāngcái shuō de nàge cí shì shénme yìsi ?
㉚ 保罗：老师，您 刚才 说 的 那个 词 是什么意思?

Paul: Mr. X, what is the meaning of that last thing
　　　you said?

Lǎoshī： Ò， shì zhèyàng de ...
老师：哦，是 这样 的……

Teacher: Oh, this is…

zěnme xiě
怎么写 how do you write
zěnme dú
怎么读 how do you say
zěnme yòng
怎么 用 how do you use
shēngdiào shì shénme
声调 是 什么 what is the intonation of

Bǎoluó: Lǎoshī，máfan nín xiě yíxià zhège zì de pīnyīn
㉛ 保罗：老师，麻烦您写一下这个字的拼音。

Paul: Mr. X, can you write down the pinyin
     for this character, please?

Lǎoshī :   Méi wèntí .
老师：没问题。

Teacher: No problem.

bǐhuà
笔画 strokes
shēngdiào
声 调 intonation
yìsi
意思 meaning

Bǎoluó： Lǎoshī， jīntiān de zuòyè shì shénme?
㉜ 保罗： 老师，今天的 <u>作业</u> 是 什么？

Paul: Mr. X, what is today's
<u>homework</u>?

Lǎoshī： Qǐng jì yíxià ...
老师： 请 记一下……
Teacher: Please take this down.

nèiróng
内容 content
zhòngdiǎn
重点 focus
nándiǎn
难点 difficulty
liànxí
练习 exercise
sīkǎotí
思考题 question

③③ Bǎoluó: Lǎoshī, wǒ māma lái Zhōngguó le, wǒ jīntiān děi xiān zǒu
保罗：老师，我妈妈来 中国 了，我今天得先 走
yíhuìr.
一会儿。

Paul: Mr. X, my mother is visiting China,
so I need to leave a bit earlier.

Lǎoshī: Hǎo, kuài qù ba.
老师： 好， 快去吧。
Teacher: Okay, hurry along.

zǎo
早 early

bàba
爸爸 father
gēge
哥哥 older brother
dìdi
弟弟 younger brother
jiějie
姐姐 older sister
mèimei
妹妹 younger sister
shūshu
叔叔 paternal uncle
bóbo
伯伯 paternal uncle
jiùju
舅舅 maternal uncle
yímā
姨妈 maternal aunt
péngyou
朋友 friend
tóngxué
同学 classmate
tóngshì
同事 colleague

老师，我妈妈来中国了，我今天得先走一会儿。

好，快去吧。

③ Bǎoluó: Míngtiān wǒ xiǎng qǐng ge jià, péi tā tā zài Běijīng
保罗: 明天 我 想 请 个假，陪她（他） 在 北京
zhuànzhuan.
转转。

Paul: I'd like to take leave tomorrow and show her (him) around Beijing.

xuéxiào
学校 the school
fùjìn
附近 the neighborhood
jiēshang
街上 the streets
nàoshìqū
闹市区 downtown
jǐ gè jǐngdiǎn
几个景点 some tourist spots

Lǎoshī: Xíng a.
老师: 行啊。

Teacher: No problem.

Bǎoluó: Xièxie nín! Lǎoshī, hòutiān jiàn.

③⑤ 保罗：谢谢您！老师，后天见。

Paul: Thank you! <u>See you the day after tomorrow</u>, Mr. X.

Lǎoshī: Zàijiàn!

老师：再见！

Teacher: Bye!

> zàijiàn
> 再见 Goodbye
> xīngqīsān jiàn
> 星期三 见 See you on Wednesday
> xià xīngqī （zhōu） jiàn
> 下星期（周）见 See you next week
> huítóu jiàn
> 回头见 See you next time

Fashion

The basic fashion principle of the Chinese university student is to look smart, stylish, and different. The colorfully clad students on campus dress according to their own interpretation of beauty, showing off their own individual tastes and styles. The most popular outfit of the university student is a pair of jeans, skater shoes, and a T-shirt. According to a survey, 80% of university students say comfort and style are the two most important factors when it comes to buying clothes, and they prefer to buy their clothes from brand name stores or vendors.

Bǎoluó : Qǐngwèn wàiwén yuèlǎnshì zài nǎr ?
㊱ 保罗 ： 请问 外文 阅览室在 哪儿？

Paul: Excuse me, where is the foreign
books reading room?

Guǎnlǐyuán : Zuǒzhuǎn shàng lóutī ， zài èr lóu .
管理员 ： 左转 上 楼梯，在二楼 .
Librarian: Take a left and go up the stairs.
It's on the second floor.

zhōngwén yuèlǎnshì
中文 阅览室 Chinese books reading
room
diànzǐ yuèlǎnshì
电子阅览室 electronic reading room
yīnxiàng yuèlǎnshì
音像 阅览室 media room
qīkānshì
期刊室 periodical room
cháxúnchù
查询处 information desk
jièyuèchù
借阅处 check-out desk

Bǎoluó： Wǒ xiǎng jiè zhè liǎng běn shū， zhè shì shūmíng .
㊲ 保罗：我想借这两本书，这是书名。

Paul: I'd like to borrow these two books. These are the titles.

Guǎnlǐyuán： Qǐng shāo děng .
管理员：请稍等。

Librarian: Just a moment, please.

Bǎoluó: Wǒ kěyǐ jiè duō cháng shíjiān?

③⑧ 保罗：我可以借多 长 时间？

Paul: How long can I borrow them?

guǎnlǐyuán: Yí gè yuè.

管理员：一个月。

Librarian: One month.

Yí gè xīngqī
一个星期 One week
Shí tiān
10 天 Ten days
Bàn gè yuè
半个月 Half a month
Yí gè bàn yuè
一个 半 月 One month and a half
Bàn nián
半 年 Half a year
Yì nián
一年 One year
Yì nián bàn
一年 半 One year and a half

Bǎoluó: Hànyǔ hěn yǒu yìsi , búguò, yě hěn nán.
㊴ 保罗：汉语 很 有意思，不过，也很 难。

Paul: Chinese is very inter-esting, but it's also very difficult.

yǒuqù
有趣 interesting
yǒu yòng
有 用 useful

Zhēnzhīzǐ: Qǐng ge jiājiào ba.
真知子： 请 个 家教 吧。

Machiko: Why don't you find a tutor?

Bǎoluó: Wǒ de Zhōngguó péngyou bù duō. Nǐ néng bāng wǒ
④⓪ 保罗: 我 的 中国 朋友 不多。 你 能 帮 我
jièshào yí gè ma?
介绍一个吗?

Paul: I don't have many Chinese friends. Can you recommend a tutor for me?

Zhēnzhīzǐ: Yuànyì xiàoláo.
真知子: 愿意 效劳。
Machiko: I'd be happy to.

Hǎo de
好 的 Sure
Xíng
行 Sure
Nà hái yòng shuō
那还用 说 You bet

我的中国朋友不多。你能帮我介绍一个吗?

愿意效劳。

The Reason for Being Late

Peter Wang is always late for class and today he's late again, so the teacher has decided to talk with him.

"Peter, why are you always late lately?"

"I've been in very poor health."

"Really? What's the matter?"

"I'm in pain all the time and I often go into shock!"

"Oh, is it that serious?"

"Of course, it is. I go into shock at 10:30 pm and don't recover until 8 am the next morning!"

"......"

Bǎoluó: Lǎoshī, shénme shíhou kǎoshì?
㊶ 保罗：老师，什么 时候 考试？

Paul: When do we have our exams?

Lǎoshī: Xià xīngqīsì, qǐng rènzhēn zhǔnbèi.
老师：下星期四，请 认真 准备。

Teacher: Next Thursday. Be sure to study hard.

qīzhōng kǎoshì
期中考试 midterm exam
qīmò kǎoshì
期末考试 final exam
suítáng kǎoshì
随堂考试 pop quiz
xiǎo cèyàn
小测验 test

Bǎoluó： Nán ma? Kǒushì háishi bǐshì ?

㊷ 保罗： 难 吗？ 口试 还是 笔试？

Paul: Will it be hard? Is it going to be an oral exam or a written exam?

Lǎoshī： Kǒushì jiā bǐshì .

老师： 口试加笔试。

Teacher: It's going to be an oral and written exam.

Bǎoluó:　Xuéxí bàogào shénme shíhou jiāo ne?
㊸ 保罗：学习报告 什么 时候 交呢?

Paul: When do we have to turn in our study reports?

Lùnwén
论文 thesis; research papers
Diàochá bàogào
调查 报告 survey reports
Dúshū bǐjì
读书笔记 book reports

Lǎoshī:　Qīmò kǎoshì yǐqián jiù xíng.
老师：期末考试 以前就行。

Teacher: Anytime before the final exam is fine.

Bǎoluó : Zhège xuéqī shénme shíhou jiéshù ?

㊹ 保罗 : 这个学期什么 时候结束?

Paul: When does this semester end?

Mǎlì : Yī yuè shíwǔ hào fàng hánjià .

玛丽 : 1 月 15 号 放 寒假。

Mary: Winter vacation starts on January 15.

㊺

Bǎoluó： Hánjià duō cháng shíjiān?
保罗： 寒假 多 长 时间？

Paul: How long is it?

Mǎlì ： Dàgài yí gè bàn yuè.
玛丽： 大概一个半月。

Mary: About a month and a half.

Dàyuē yí gè bàn yuè
大约一个半月
About a month and a half
Yí gè bàn yuè zuǒyòu
一个半月左右
About a month and a half
Chàbuduō yí gè bàn yuè
差不多一个半月
About a month and a half

The Student Cafeteria

Chinese university students come from all around the country and they all have different tastes. Whether or not they can find something they like to eat can be a problem. In light of this, universities often have other specialty cafeterias besides the main one, and students can find what they like among the variety of cuisines offered at these alternative places. Some schools even have restaurants that specialize in western cuisine or Muslim cuisine, and offer a choice of cafes or bars, allowing both Chinese and foreign students a variety of choices.

Bǎoluó: Wǒ péngyou xiǎng shēnqǐng wàiguó liúxuéshēng jiǎngxuéjīn,
㊻ 保罗: 我 朋友 想 申请 外国 留学生 奖学金,
xūyào shénme shǒuxù?
需要 什么 手续?

Paul: My friend wants to apply for
a foreign student scholarship.
What does he need to do?

> gōngdú shuòshì xuéwèi
> 攻读 硕士 学位 a Master's program
> gōngdú bóshì xuéwèi
> 攻读 博士 学位 a PhD program
> cānjiā wàiguórén shuō Hànyǔ bǐsài
> 参加外国人 说汉语比赛
> taking part in a Chinese speaking
> contest for foreigners

Lǎoshī: Yào xiān tiánxiě yí fèn shēnqǐngbiǎo.
老师: 要 先 填写 一份 申请表。

Teacher: First he needs to fill out an application form.

Bǎoluó: Hái xūyào shénme cáiliào ma?

㊼ 保罗: 还需要什么 材料 吗？

Paul: Does he need to submit other material?

Lǎoshī: Zìwǒ píngjià, chéngjìdān, liǎng fēng lǎoshī de tuījiànxìn,

老师: 自我评价、成绩单、两 封 老师的推荐信、

fābiǎo lùnwén de xiāngguān zīliào, háiyǒu cānjiā xiàonèi-wài

发表论文的 相关 资料，还有参加 校内外

huódòng de zīliào děng.

活动 的资料 等。

Teacher: He will need to submit a self-review, transcripts
for all institutions he's attended, two letters of
recommendation, information concerning papers
he's published, and information on his extracur-
ricular activities.

Bǎoluó: Cáiliào jiāogěi shuí?
48 保罗： 材料 交给 谁？

Paul: Where should he submit the material?

Lǎoshī: Gěi Yáng lǎoshī jiù kěyǐ le， tā de diànhuà shì
老师： 给 杨 老师就可以了，她的 电话 是
liù wǔ qī qī jiǔ sān wǔ jiǔ.
6 5 7 7 9 3 5 9。

Teacher: He can give it to Ms. Yang. Her number is 65779359.

Bǎoluó: Lǎoshī, wǒ xiǎng kāi yì zhāng zhèngmíng.

㊾ 保罗：老师，我 想 开一 张 ___证明___。

Paul: Mr. X, I'd like to have a <u>certificate</u>.

Lǎoshī: Hǎo de. qǐngshāoděng, wǒ qù zhǎo
老师： 好的。请 稍 等，我去找
xìzhǔrèn qiān zì, gài zhāng.
系主任 签字、盖 章。

Teacher: Okay. Just a moment. I will get the signature of the head of department and stamp.

jièshàoxìn
介绍信 letter of recommendation

jiàtiáo
假条 leave permit

Bǎoluó： Máfannín le .
㊿ 保罗： 麻烦您了。

Paul: Thank you.

Lǎoshī： Bú kèqi .
老师： 不客气。

Teacher: You're welcome.

Student Apartments

Chinese universities usually provide apartments for students either on or off campus. Undergraduate rooms typically house 4-6 people per room, while Master's student rooms house 2-3 per room and PhD student rooms 1-2 per room. Men and women usually occupy different buildings, but sometimes they are in the same building and just in separately managed quarters. Every apartment has an on-duty office and guest area on the first floor that are managed by school staff. Rooms are equipped with beds, desks, closets, bookcases, and washrooms. Students can study, get online, and watch TV in their rooms. It is a pretty convenient setup.

Xuéwèi hé Wénpíng
10. 学位和文凭 Degrees and Diplomas

Bǎoluó： Lǎoshī， wǒ xiǎng bàokǎo shuòshì yánjiūshēng.
(51) 保罗：老师，我 想 报考 硕士 研究生。

Paul: Mr. X, I'd like to apply for the Master's program.

Lǎoshī： Hǎo a， zhè shì jiǎnzhāng.
老师：好啊，这 是 简章。

Teacher: OK. Here's a brochure explaining the application procedures.

běnkē
本科 undergraduate program
bóshì yánjiūshēng
博士研究生 PhD program
bóshìhòu
博士后 post doctoral program

Bǎoluó： Bàomíngbiǎo ne？
(52) 保罗： 报名表 呢？

Paul: How about the application form?

Lǎoshī： Yào cóng xuéyuànwǎng shang xiàzǎi .
老师：要 从 学院 网 上 下载。

Teacher: You can download it from the school's webpage.

Bǎoluó: Wǎngzhǐ shì ...
(53) 保罗： 网址 是……

Paul: What's the website?

Lǎoshī: Zài zhèr .
老师：在这儿。

Teacher: It's right here.

Bìyè Diǎnlǐ hé Jiéyè Diǎnlǐ

11. 毕业典礼和结业典礼

Commencement and Graduation

Bǎoluó: Zhōngyú bìyè le!

(54) 保罗：终于毕业了！

Paul: I've finally graduated!

> jiéyè
> 结业
> completed the program
> wánchéng xuéyè
> 完成 学业
> finished my studies

Tóngxué: Shì a, zhēn bù róngyì a!

同学：是啊，真不容易啊！

Classmate: Yes you have. You've earned it!

Bǎoluó : Bìyè yǐhòu , nǐ yǒu shénme dǎsuàn?
(55) 保罗：毕业以后，你有 什么 打算？

Paul: What do you want to do after graduation?

jìhuà
计划 plans do you have
ānpái
安排 do you have arranged
xiǎngfǎ
想法 ideas do you have

Tóngxué : Wǒ děi huí guó zhǎo gōngzuò . Nǐ ne ?
同学：我得回国 找 工作。你呢？

Classmate: I have to find a job back home. How about you?

jiéhūn
结婚 get married
jìxù dúshū
继续读书 continue with my studies
bāngzhù fùmǔ dǎlǐ gōngsī
帮助 父母打理公司
help run the family business

Bǎoluó: Wǒ dǎsuàn liú zài zhèlǐ dú yánjiūshēng.
(56) 保罗：我打算留在这里读研究生。

Paul: I plan to stay here and go to graduate school.

Tóngxué: Dú wán yánjiūshēng, nǐ jiù chéng "Zhōngguótōng" la!
同学：读完研究生，你就成"中国通"啦！

Classmate: After graduate school you'll become an old China hand!

Bǎoluó： Nǎlǐ ， nǎlǐ .
⑤⑦ 保罗 ：哪里，哪里。

Paul: Not at all.

Guò jiǎng le
过 奖 了 Not at all
Bié kāi wánxiào le
别开玩笑了 Stop joking (come on)
Dànyuàn ba
但愿 吧 I hope so

哪里，哪里。

Yuànzhǎng： Zhùhè nǐ！
院长 ：祝贺你！
Dean: Congratulations!

Gōngxǐ nǐ
恭喜你
Congratulations

Bǎoluó： Xièxie nín， xièxie xuéxiào de péiyǎng！
(58) 保罗：谢谢您，谢谢学校的培养！
Paul: Thank you and I'd like to thank the school for cultivating me.

lǎoshī
老师 teachers

At the Graduation Ceremony

The president was calling the name of the student who was first in his graduating class to come up and receive his award. The student didn't walk on stage until his name had been called several times. After the ceremony, a teacher approached the student and asked, " What happened? Were you sick or did you not hear your name?" "No, I wasn't sick," the student replied, "I just wanted to make sure the other students heard my name."

第三部分　生活篇
Part 3 Student Life

Bǎoluó： Yìqǐ chūqù chī fàn ba .
⑤⑨ 保罗： 一起出去 吃饭吧。

Paul: Let's go out to eat.

Péngyou： Hǎo a .
朋友： 好啊。

Friend: Sure.

hē chá
喝茶 for a cup of tea
hē jiǔ
喝酒 for a drink
pào ba
泡吧 to a bar
cuō yí dùn
撮一顿 for a big meal

Péngyou： Lùkǒu xīn kāile yì jiā xiǎochīdiàn，
朋友：路口新开了一家小吃店，
zánmen qù chángchang？
咱们去 尝尝 ？

shìshi
试试 try it out
kànkan
看看 take a look
qiáoqiao
瞧瞧 take a look

Friend: There's a newly opened restaurant at the corner of the road. Do you want to give it a try?

Bǎoluó： Yǒu shénme hǎo chī de ma？
(60) 保罗：有什么好吃的吗？

Paul: What's there to eat?

Péngyou： Tīngshuō dōu shì yìxiē lǎo Běijīng xiǎochī .
朋友： 听说 都是一些老 北京 小吃。

Friend: I heard it's all old Beijing snack food.

Bǎoluó： Zhēn de？ Tài bàng le！
� 保罗： 真的? 太 棒 了!

Paul: Really? That's great!

Péngyou： Zǒu， jīntiān wǒ qǐng kè .
朋友： 走，今天我 请客。

màidān
买单
I'll pay the bill

Friend: Let's go. My treat today.

听说都是
一些老北
京小吃。

真的? 太棒了!

走，今天我请客。

Bǎoluó: Nà bùxíng, háishi AA zhì ba.
(62) 保罗：那不行，还是 AA 制吧。

Paul: No, let's split the cost.

wǒ qǐng nǐ
我请你 It's on me.

Chōng Zhí hé Mǎi Kǎ
2. 充值和买卡 Buying Minutes and Cards

Bǎoluó: Wǒ de fànkǎ li kuài méi qián le.
(63) 保罗：我的饭卡里快没钱了。

Paul: My meal card is almost out of money.

diànhuàkǎ 电话卡 telephone card
gōngjiāokǎ 公交卡 bus card
měishíkǎ 美食卡 food card
diànkǎ 电卡 electricity card
shuǐkǎ 水卡 water card
méiqìkǎ 煤气卡 gas card

Gōngzuò rényuán: Chōng duōshao?
工作人员：充多少？

Staff: How much do you want to add?

Mǎi 买 buy

64 Bǎoluó: Yìbǎi kuài qián de ba .
保罗：100 块 钱 的吧。

Paul: 100 yuan.

Gōngzuò rényuán: Chōnghǎo le ， gěi nǐ kǎ .
工作 人员： 充 好 了，给 你 卡。

Staff: All done. Here's your card.

Bǎoluó: Yǒu shǒujī chōngzhíkǎ ma?
⑥⑤ 保罗: 有 手机 充值卡 吗?

Paul: Do you sell prepaid cell phone cards?

Shòuhuòyuán: Yǒu. Yào nǎ zhǒng de?
售货员 : 有。要 哪 种 的?

Salesperson: Yes. What kind would you like?

㉞ Bǎoluó： Quánqiútōngkǎ.

⑥ 保罗： 全球 通卡。

Paul: The GoTone card.

Shénzhōuxínggkǎ
神州 行卡 Easyown card
Dònggǎn didàikà
动感 地带卡 M-Zone card
Liántōngkǎ
联通卡 Unicom card

Shòuhuòyuán： Yào duōshao miànzhí de？
售货员 ： 要 多少 面值 的?

Salesperson: Which value card would you like?

Bǎoluó: Wǔshí yuán yì zhāng de .
㉖ 保罗： 50 元一张 的。

Paul: I'd like the 50 yuan one.

Yībǎi yuán
100 元 100 yuan
Èrbǎi yuán
200 元 200 yuan
Sānbǎi yuán
300 元 300 yuan

Shòuhuòyuán: Yào jǐ zhāng?
售货员 ： 要几张？

Salesperson: How many cards?

Bǎoluó: Lái yì zhāng ba .
⑱ 保罗：来一 张 吧。

Paul: One , please.

liǎng zhāng
两 张 Two
sān zhāng
三 张 Three

Student Clubs

Chinese university students are not just into studying. They participate in a number of other activities as well. Besides regular classes, students can also participate in workshops, forums, academic lectures, recreational activities, and joint-school activities. Universities also host art festivals, athletic meets, and other athletic competitions for students during spring and fall. In addition, students have the option of joining different clubs, such as choir, drama, dance, literature, chess, and photography clubs. There are also student-led volunteer activities that encourage people to volunteer their time to help communities.

Bǎoluó: Nǎr kěyǐ xǐ yīfu？
⑥⑨ 保罗： 哪儿可以洗衣服？

Paul: Where can I do laundry?

Fúwùyuán: Xǐyījiān yǒu gōngyòng xǐyījī.
服务员：洗衣间有 公用 洗衣机。

Staff: There are public washers in the laundry room.

⑦ Bǎoluó : Zěnme yòng ne ?
保罗： 怎么 用呢?

Paul: How do I use them?

Fúwùyuán : Miǎnfèi shǐyòng .
服务员： <u>免费 使用</u> 。

Staff: <u>They're free</u>.

Xūyào tóu bì
需要投币
They're coin operated.

Bǎoluó: Xuéxiào yǒu gānxǐdiàn ma?
⑦ 保罗：学校 有 干洗店 吗？

Paul: Does the school have a dry cleaner's?

Fúwùyuán: Chāoshì dōngbian yǒu yì jiā.
服务员：超市 <u>东边</u> 有一家。

Staff: There's one <u>east of</u> the supermarket.

xībian
西边 west of
nánbian
南边 south of
běibian
北边 north of
qiánbian
前边 in front of
hòubian
后边 behind
zuǒbian
左边 on the left of
yòubian
右边 on the right of

Bǎoluó : Wǒ xiǎng mǎi diǎnr shēnghuó yòngpǐn.
⑫ 保罗 : 我 想 买 点儿 生活 用品。

Paul: I need to buy some daily supplies.

Péngyou : Nǐ qù xuéxiào chāoshì ba , dōngxi hěn quán.
朋友 : 你 去 学校 超市 吧，东西 很 全。

Friend: You can go to the school supermarket. They have everything.

rìyòngpǐn
日用品 daily supplies
chī de
吃的 food
yǐnliào
饮料 drinks
yào
药 medicine
wénjù
文具 writing utensils

duō
多 a lot of things
hǎo
好 good stuff
piányi
便宜 cheap prices
shíhuì
实惠 good prices

Bǎoluó: Yàoshi mǎi shuǐguǒ qù nǎr hǎo?
73 保罗： 要是 买 水果 去 哪儿 好？

Paul: Where is the best place to buy fruit?

Péngyou: Qù shuǐguǒtānr ba, yòu piányi yòu xīnxiān.
朋友： 去 水果 摊儿 吧， 又 便宜 又 新鲜。

Friend: Go to a fruit stall. The fruit there is cheap and fresh.

Teacher's Day

Teachers have always been highly respected in Chinese culture. On January 21, 1985, to show respect to teachers, China declared September 10 to be Teacher's Day. Teachers around the country celebrate this day in different ways, and people thank their teachers in different ways, too, such as by giving them flowers or small gifts.

87

Bǎoluó : Lái píng kělè .
⑦⑷ 保罗 ： 来 瓶 <u>可乐</u>。

Paul: A bottle of
<u>Coke</u>, please.

Shòuhuòyuán : Yào bīng de ma?
售货员 ： 要 冰 的 吗?

Salesperson: Refrigerated?

xuěbì
雪碧 Sprite
kuàngquánshuǐ
矿泉水 mineral water
hóngchá
红茶 black tea
chéngzhī
橙汁 orange juice
lǜchá
绿茶 green tea
guǒzhī
果汁 juice
xiānchéngduō
鲜橙多 Xianchengduo
orange juice
píjiǔ
啤酒 beer

Bǎoluó:　Chángwēn de．　Duōshao qián?
⑦⑤ 保罗：　常温 的。　多少 钱？

Paul: Room temperature. How much?

Shòuhuòyuán：　Wǔ kuài．
售货员　：　5 块。

Salesperson: 5 yuan.

Bǎoluó:　Zhèr yǒu Yīngwén bàozhǐ ma?

⑦ 保罗：这儿有 英文 报纸 吗?

zázhì
杂志 magazines

Paul: Do you sell English language <u>newspapers</u> here?

Shòuhuòyuán:　Duìbuqǐ, méiyǒu. Nǐ qù nàbian de bàotānr

售货员 ：对不起，没有。你去那边的报摊儿

kànkan ba.

看看吧。

Salesperson: Sorry, we don't. Maybe you can try the newspaper stand over there.

⑦ Bǎoluó： Wǒ xiǎng jiǎnjian tóufa .
保罗： 我 想 剪剪头发。

Paul: I'd like to get a haircut.

Lǐfàshī ： Huānyíng， qǐng zuò ba .
理发师： 欢迎 ， 请 坐 吧。

Stylist: Welcome. Please take a seat.

xiūxiu
修修 trim
tàngtang
烫烫 perm

⑦8 Bǎoluó： Nǐ juéde wǒ zuò shénmeyàng de fàxíng bǐjiào hǎo?
保罗： 你觉得我 做 什么样 的发型比较好？

Paul: What kind of hairstyle do you think would suit me?

Lǐfàshī： Kànkan shūshang yǒu méiyǒu nǐ xǐhuan de yàngshì.
理发师： 看看 书上 有 没有你喜欢的 样式。

Stylist: Take a look at the book and see if there's anything you like.

Bǎoluó:　Nín bāng wǒ shèjì　yí gè ba.
⑦⑨ 保罗：　您 帮 我 设计 一个 吧。

Paul: Why don't you design something for me?

Lǐfàshī　:　Hǎo.　Xiān xǐxi tóu ba.
理发师：　好。 先 洗洗头 吧。

Stylist: Sure. Let's wash your hair first.

Something Exciting

It was the beginning of the semester and the students were waiting for their new Chinese teacher to arrive. The teacher finally came and he turned out to be a very handsome young man. A girl in the class, feeling in a flirtatious mood, asked, "Why don't we forget about class and do something exciting instead?" "Okay," said the teacher, after giving the suggestion some thought. "Put away your books and get ready for an exam!"

Bǎoluó： Wǒ yǒudiǎnr bù shūfu .
⑧⓪ 保罗： 我 有点儿 不 舒服。

Paul: I don't feel well.

Yīshēng： Nǐ qù nèikē zhǎo dàifu kànkan ba .
医生： 你去 内科 找 大夫 看看 吧。

Doctor: Maybe you can go see an internist.

Yīshēng： Zěnme le ?
医生： 怎么了？

Doctor: What seems to be the matter?

⑧ Bǎoluó： Wǒ zhè liǎng tiān sǎngzi téng .
   保罗： 我 这 两 天 嗓子 疼。

Paul: I've had a sore throat for

the past couple of days.

tóu téng
头 疼 had a headache
tóu yūn
头 晕 been dizzy
késou
咳嗽 had a cough
fāshāo
发烧 had a fever
xīn huāng
心 慌 had palpitations
wèi téng
胃 疼 had a stomachache
dǔzi téng
肚子疼 had abdominal pain

Yīshēng： Wǒ kànkan .
医生： 我 看看。

Doctor: Let's take a look.

怎么了？

我这两天嗓子疼。

我看看。

Yīshēng： Méi shénme dà wèntí， chī diǎnr yào jiù néng hǎo.
医生： 没 什么 大问题，吃点儿药就 能 好。

Doctor: It's nothing serious. Some medication will do the trick.

Bǎoluó： Nà wǒ jiù fàngxīn le .
⑧② 保罗：那 我 就 放心 了。

Paul: That's good to know.

Yīshēng: Gěi nǐ yàofāng qù ná yào ba.
医生：给你药方去拿药吧。

Doctor: Here's the prescription.

Bǎoluó: Hái yào zhùyì shénme ma?
㉝ 保罗：还要注意什么 吗?

Paul: Is there anything else I should know?

Yīshēng: Yídìng yào ànshí chī yào, bié chī yóunì de shíwù.
医生：一定要按时吃药，别吃油腻的食物。

Doctor: Remember to take your medication regularly and don't eat anything oily.

bù hǎo xiāohuà de
不好 消化的
hard to digest
xīnlà de
辛辣的 spicy
tài yìng de
太硬的 too
difficult to chew

给你药方
去拿药吧。

还要注意什
么吗?

一定要按时
吃药，别吃
油腻的食物。

Bǎoluó:　Qǐngwèn nǎge chuāngkǒu kěyǐ huàn qián?
⑧ 保罗：　请问　哪个　窗口　可以　换　钱？

Paul: Which window can I go
to for currency exchange?

Jīnglǐ：　Qǐng dào liù hào chuāngkǒu.
经理：　请　到 6 号　窗口。

Manager: Please go to window
No. 6.

cún qián
存钱 make a deposit
qǔ qián
取钱 draw cash
huì kuǎn
汇款 make a transfer
guàshī
挂失 report a lost card
bàn jièjìkǎ
办借记卡 apply for a debit card
bàn xìnyòngkǎ
办信用卡 apply for a credit card

请问哪个窗口可
以换钱？

请到 6
号窗口。

Guìyuán: Nín hǎo! Nín bànlǐ shénme yèwù?
柜员: 您 好! 您办理什么 业务?

Clerk: Hello. What can I do for you today?

Xūyào bāngmáng ma
需要 帮 忙 吗
Do you need help

Wǒ néng bāng nín ma
我 能 帮 您 吗
Can I help you

Bǎoluó: Wǒ xiǎng huàn xiē Rénmínbì.
⑧⑤ 保罗: 我 想 换 些 人民币。

Paul: I'd like to exchange some US dollars for RMB.

Guìyuán: Huàn duōshao?
柜员： 换 多少？

Clerk: How much would you like to exchange?

⑧⑥ Bǎoluó: Wǔbǎi měiyuán.
保罗： 500 美元。

Paul: 500 US dollars.

Guìyuán: Hǎo de. Qǐng shāo děng.
柜员： 好的。 请 稍 等。

děng yihuìr
等一会儿
Wait a second

Clerk: No problem. Just a moment, please.

换多少？

500 美元。

好的。
请稍
等。

Bǎoluó： Zài máfan nín huàn yìdiǎnr língqián.
⑧⑦ 保罗： 再 麻烦您 换一点儿 零钱。

Paul: Could I also get some smaller
bills, please?

新钱 new bills
xīn qián

Guìyuán : Duō dà miànzhí de ?
柜 员 ： 多 大 面 值 的？

Clerk: How small?

Bǎoluó : Shí kuài， èrshí kuài de dōu xíng .
⑧⑧ 保罗： 10 块、 20 块的 都 行。

Paul: Either 10 or 20 RMB bills would be fine.

Part-time Jobs

It is very common for Chinese university students to find part-time jobs, and working part-time has become a very important part of their college lives. Part-time jobs provide students with more connections, a livelier college life, and a chance to use what they've learned in the community, not to mention it is also the main source of their spending money. Working part-time gives students a chance to enter society, hone their skills, and build their experience and professional knowledge; it can also lessen the financial burden of the family and allow them to learn how to manage their money.

8. 参加 学生 社团 Joining Student Clubs

Zhōngguó xuésheng： Xuésheng shètuán zhāo xīn ，huānyíng bàomíng！

中国　学生：　学生　社团　招新，欢迎　报名！

Chinese student: Student clubs are now recruiting new members. Please feel free to sign up!

Bǎoluó： Wǒ kěyǐ cānjiā shètuán ma？

⑧⑨ 保罗：我可以参加 社团 吗？

Paul: Can I join a student club?

Zhōngguó xuésheng： Dāngrán kěyǐ ！

中国　学生：　当然 可以！

Chinese student: Of course!

Bǎoluó: Wǒ xiǎng cānjiā héchàngtuán, xíng ma?
⑨ 保罗：我 想 参加 合唱团 ，行 吗？

Paul: I'd like to join the choir. Is that okay?

huàjùtuán
话剧团 drama club
wǔdǎotuán
舞蹈团 dance club
wénxuéshè
文学社 literature club
qíyìshè
棋艺社 chess club
shèyǐngshè
摄影社 photography club
měigōngshè
美工社 art club
lánqiúduì
篮球队 basketball team
zúqiúduì
足球队 soccer team

Zhōngguó xuésheng: Huānyíng huānyíng!
中国 学生：欢迎 欢迎！

Chinese student: Of course. Welcome!

我想参加合唱团，行吗？

欢迎 欢迎！

Bǎoluó： Zhōumò zánmen qù nǎr wánr？
⑨1 保罗： 周末 咱们去哪儿玩儿？

Paul: Where should we go for the weekend?

Péngyou： Qù guàng jiē ba． Wǒ zhīdào
朋友： 去 逛 街 吧。 我 知 道
yǒu ge dìfang tè bàng．
有 个 地 方 特 棒 。

Friend: Let's go shopping. I know
a great place.

kàn diànyǐng
看 电影 to the movies
guàng shūdiàn
逛 书店 to the bookstore
pào wǎngbā
泡 网吧 to an internet cafe
bèngdí
蹦迪 disco dancing
K gē
K 歌 to a KTV

Bǎoluó： Zánmen dǎ chē qù ma?

㉒ 保罗： 咱们 **打车去吗**?

Paul: Are we <u>taking a taxi</u>?

zuò gōngjiāochē
坐 公交 车 taking a bus
qí chē
骑车 riding our bicycles
zǒuzhe
走着 walking

Péngyou： Háishi zuò dìtiě bǐjiào fāngbiàn.

朋友： 还是 坐 地铁比较 方便。

Friend: I think the subway would be more convenient.

Bǎoluó: Jǐ diǎn jiànmiàn?
⑨ 保罗：几点 见面？

Paul: What time do you want to meet?

Péngyou: Sì diǎn, xuéxiào nánmén.
朋友：4点，学校 南门。

Friend: Four o'clock. At the south gate.

Bǎoluó: Hǎo, bújiàn-búsàn!
94 保罗：好，不见不散！

Paul: Okay. See you there!

Visiting Your Teacher

If you study in China, there will be many opportunities to visit a Chinese home, especially your teacher's home. Many of the customs in China are the same as in other countries when it comes to paying a visit. For example, you need to be on time, bring a little something, and thank your hosts for having you. If you don't know what to bring, fruit, flowers or candies are always good choices. If the family has children or elderly family members, then the host will be just as happy if you only brought gifts for them. Usually, as a guest, you would want to leave before dinner. Though your hosts will often insist on keeping you, it is usually an inconvenience for them unless they have already invited you in advance.

Zhōngguó péngyou : Bǎoluó， nǐ de shēncái zhēn bàng！
中国　朋友：保罗，你的身材　真　棒！

Chinese friend: Paul, you look really fit!

Bǎoluó : Nà dāngrán， wǒ měitiān dōu duànliàn.
⑨⑤ 保罗：那 当然，我 每天 都 锻炼。

Paul: That's for sure. I work out every day.

Zhōngguó péngyou: Zài nǎr liàn? wǒ yě xiǎng duànliàn duànliàn ne .

中国　朋友：在哪儿练? 我也 想　锻炼　锻炼 呢。

Chinese friend: Where? I'd like
　　　　　　to work out, too.

Bǎoluó: Xuéxiào de jiànshēnfáng a!

⑨⑥ 保罗：学校的 健身房 啊!

Paul: At the school gym.

cāochǎng
操场　track field

yùndòngchǎng
运动场　sports arena

yóuyǒngguǎn
游泳馆　swimming pool

wǎngqiúchǎng
网球场　tennis court

lánqiúchǎng
篮球场 basketball court

páiqiúchǎng
排球场　volleyball court

zúqiúchǎng
足球场 soccer field

yǔmáoqiúguǎn
羽毛球馆 badminton court

pīngpāngqiúshì
乒乓球室 table tennis room

在哪儿练? 我也
想锻炼锻炼呢。

学校的健
身房啊!

Zhōngguó péngyou: Xià cì qù duànliàn jiàoshàng wǒ, xíng ma?
中国　朋友：下次去 锻炼 叫上 我，行 吗？

Chinese friend: Can you let me know the next time you go?

Bǎoluó: Hǎowa, míngtiān wǒ jiù dài nǐ qù!
⑰ 保罗：好哇，明天 我就带你去！

Paul: Sure! I'll take you there tomorrow.

Bǎoluó： Dàjiā jiāyóu a , lí bǐsài hái yǒu liǎng tiān le .
⑨⑧ 保罗： 大家加油啊，离比赛还有 两 天 了。

Paul: Let's go, everyone! There's only
two days left until the game.

juésài
决赛 the final games
chūsài
初赛 the first round
xuǎnbásài
选拔赛 the
preliminary round
fùsài
复赛 the second round

Tóngxué： Tīngshuō Zhōngguó tóngxué tè
同学： 听说 中国 同学 特
lìhai , wǒmen néng yíng ma?
厉害，我们 能 赢 吗?

Classmate: I hear our Chinese classmates are amazing.
Can we beat them?

Bǎoluó： Děngzhe qiáo ba .

⑨⑨ 保罗： 等 着 瞧 吧。

Paul: Let's just wait and see!

Bǎoluó: Lǎoshī, zhè xuéqī xuéxiào zǔzhī lǚxíng ma?
⑩ 保罗：老师，这学期学校组织旅行吗？

Paul: Mr. X, has the school organized any trips this semester?

jiāoyóu
郊游 outings
cānguān
参观 visits
huódòng
活动 activities

Lǎoshī: Zǔzhī a, Shí-Yī qù Xī'ān.
老师：组织啊，十一去西安。

Teacher: Yes, it has. We're going to Xi'an during the October holidays.

⑩ Bǎoluó: Hǎojí le, wǒ duì Zhōngguó gǔchéng zuì gǎn xìngqù le!
保罗：好极了，我对 中国 古城 最 感 兴趣了!

Paul: Great. I'm really interested in <u>ancient Chinese cities</u>.

bīng mǎ yǒng
兵马俑 the Terracotta Warriors
pào mó
泡馍 pita bread soaked in soup

Teaching by Tape

A university professor was asked to attend an important meeting at the last minute. Because he did not want his graduate students to miss a class, he decided to tape what he was going to talk about on a cassette tape. He then asked the teaching assistant to notify the eight students that they were to come to class as scheduled and listen to his taped class. The meeting ended early, however, and the professor hurried back to class. When he walked in, nobody was there. His tape was still on though, but instead of students listening, he saw eight small cassette recorders taping his lecture from a big cassette player.

责任编辑：傅 眉
英文编辑：韩芙芸
封面设计：古 手
印刷监制：佟汉冬

图书在版编目（CIP）数据

漫画汉语 101 句．学生篇：汉英对照 / 张婧，陈晓宁编著 .—北京：华语教学出版社，2009
　ISBN 978-7-80200-628-7

Ⅰ.漫… Ⅱ.①张… ②陈… Ⅲ.汉语－口语－对外汉语教学－教材 Ⅳ.H195.4

中国版本图书馆 CIP 数据核字（2009）第 113577 号

漫画汉语 101 句（学生篇）

张婧 陈晓宁 编著
J. Y. Standaert 译
黄钧升 插图
＊
© 华语教学出版社
华语教学出版社出版
（中国百万庄大街 24 号 邮政编码 100037）
电话：(86)10-68320585
传真：(86)10-68326333
网址：www.sinolingua.com.cn
电子信箱：hyjx@sinolingua.com.cn
北京外文印刷厂印刷
2009 年（32 开）第一版
（汉英）
ISBN 978-7-80200-628-7
定价：45.00 元